LINES INTO LONDON

London Railways in the Post-War Years

WRENFORD J. THATCHER

Kings Cross Shed (Top Shed) with 60146, 60538, 60122, 60142, 60013 identified.

First published 2011

The History Press
The Mill, Brimscombe Port
Stroud, Gloucestershire, GL5 2QG
www.thehistorypress.co.uk

British Library Cataloguing in Publication Data.
A catalogue record for this book is available from the British Library.

ISBN 978 0 7524 5892 2

Typesetting and origination by The History Press
Printed in Great Britain
Manufacturing managed by Jellyfish Print Solutions Ltd

Contents

Acknowledgements

The author would like to express his thanks to the many people who have enabled this book to be written. Although the photographs came later, the many hours spent at the line side with my mother, when I was a very small child, undoubtedly encouraged my love of the steam locomotive. At the age of ninety-four she still takes an interest in my railway photography, although doubting my sanity at taking hundreds of photographs of the same steam engines (they are all alike to her!).

The time spent on the footplate of various locomotives thanks to the kindness of many engine drivers in the pre-Beeching era contributed in no small measure, and the tolerance of railway staff to the huge number of 'spotters' at the time enabled many of these photographs to be taken.

Except where stated, all the black and white photographs were taken by the author, but some of the coloured photographs were taken by Hazel Thatcher, who patiently tolerated my instructions and sometimes achieved better results by ignoring them!

I would also like to express my thanks to Adrienne Scott who was sufficiently impressed by the photography to encourage me to write a book, and to contact the publishers on my behalf. Without this I would never have started.

Finally I would like to thank Amy Rigg at The History Press for her encouragement, enthusiasm and patience.

6201 *Princess Elizabeth* at speed near Hereford.

Geographical Setting and Historical Background

Most of the readers of this book will be well aware of the boundaries of the railway companies, but some of those boundaries were quite blurred, and post-Beeching became even more so. After the Second World War the railways were in a very dilapidated state, and the Government, which had used and depended upon them for the duration of hostilities, showed no inclination to support the individual railway companies which had existed since the grouping in 1922. Those companies were the London and North Eastern (LNE), the London Midland and Scottish (LMS), the Southern (SR) and the Great Western Railways (GWR) respectively. It is interesting to note that although all of them terminated in London, only the first two referred to the fact. This may have been because the two northern lines operated so far from the capital that they saw the link to London as only a small part of their business, whereas the two southern lines had little purpose to their existence other than to link the communities they served to London. Nevertheless, the GWR had a main line which extended all the way to Penzance, which is as distant from London as Carlisle, and the sign outside Penzance station even to this day reads 'Welcome to England'! Perhaps the GWR could have been called the London and Great Western Railway instead.

So even in these early years before nationalisation in 1948, we can see how the boundaries were blurred. The GWR still competed with the SR for traffic to Devon and Cornwall, and with the LMS for traffic to Birmingham and the West Midlands. The Great Western therefore had a war on two fronts and managed to sustain hostilities with considerable success. The LNER competed with the LMS for traffic to Nottingham and the Midlands and as always for traffic to Scotland. The competition was healthy. It gave both freight and passenger customers a choice, and encouraged competitive timings and prices. It gave rise to a pride in the staff for 'their' company, and encouraged efficiency as well as service.

All this was swept away in the nationalisation of the railways in 1948, when the big four, as they were known, were amalgamated to form British Railways.

There is little doubt that many of the railwaymen wanted this. I know my own grandfathers, both drivers on the former LNER, greatly favoured the formation of the national railway. Much of this was borne from the stress of the war, the long hours and awful conditions which railway staff had to work under during those years. The promise nationalisation held out was better working conditions, shorter hours and better pay. In an ideal world it offered standardisation of equipment and working practices (a system adopted by the GWR from the times of Churchward forty years earlier!). It sounded like a good idea on paper, especially to a staff weary

Ernest Henry Thatcher with his family, *c*.1923.

after years of war. What it needed to make it work was money – a lot of money – and the cash-strapped post-war government was desperately short of money. The changes promised by nationalisation altered the attitude of the working men on the railways. The changes were slow, and the rundown railways had to continue with what they had for several years. Discontent and industrial unrest grew from a lack of progress, while at the same time memories clung to the 'good old days'. Eventually the wheel went full circle. The railways were decimated by Marples, who used a certain Dr Beeching to do his axe work. Under Thatcher and successive governments the railways were privatised, then split up and part privatised, part nationalised. At the time of writing, new railways are being constructed to replace those torn up.

It seems that the boundaries of our railway system are rather like those of Europe in the past 100 years: changing, dividing, reshaping. This book will concentrate mainly on the post-nationalisation period when the railways were split into four main regions. As an approximate guide, the Eastern and Midland operated north of the capital, either side of a line which passes through the Pennine hills to a point midway between Glasgow and Edinburgh; to the north of this was the Scottish region, which comprised a mixture of the old LMS and LNER. The other two companies operated mainly to the south of the Thames with the exception of the Western, which tenaciously operated into Birmingham. The Southern region mainly served Kent, Surrey, Sussex, Hampshire and Dorset. The Western served Wales, Cornwall, Devon, Gloucestershire, Herefordshire, Oxfordshire, parts of Warwickshire and Somerset.

The change which occurred to each railway region after nationalisation in 1948 was inevitably dictated by the history of the line before that time, so as well as the shifting of boundaries these changes were often coloured by working practices which sometimes extended back 100 years or more. My own grandfathers both worked as drivers on the Great Eastern Railway and then the London North Eastern Railway (LNER). Everything they talked about related to those railways – they never thought of British Rail as a unified body, thought everything non-Great Eastern was 'cissy' (especially the GWR!) and that the drivers from Stratford (the main GE shed) were a load of know-it-alls. They were proud of their railway, carried their railwayman's regulator (pocket watch to you and me, but it says railwayman's regulator on the back) in their weskits (waistcoats) and kept 'railway time' (i.e. what the station clock read). The picture opposite shows Ernest Henry Thatcher, railwayman, in the typical dress of the Great Eastern engine driver, complete with greasetop cap which he wore even at home. The author is the small boy in the picture, and it is easy to see how I spent much of my time on the footplate as a child! Behind the group was the garden, then a chicken run, and beyond that one could see a distant view of Bishops Stortford railway yard.

The atmosphere there was always one of excitement. Mill chimneys and roofs obscured what would have been a perfect view, and I have often regretted that no photographs seem to exist of it.

The yard at Bishops Stortford was a treat to a small boy. As a way of understanding how locality and history jointly affected the way in which the railways operated, the routine of Driver E. Thatcher gives some insight. By all accounts Ernest Henry was not an easy man on the footplate. He was gruff and demanding, yet a kinder man to his grandson could not have been imagined. He expected his fireman to do his job without comment; I think this stemmed from

Ernest Henry Thatcher on the footplate of 8028 and 8016, both at Bishops Stortford.

the time when he was involved in a shunting accident resulting in the death of a brakesman who was walking the yard at Stortford. Ernest Henry was elevated to the top link fairly late in life, but most of his time was spent on local stopping trains between Liverpool Street and Cambridge. Shown opposite is a picture of him on his footplate at Bishops Stortford. I have no date for these photographs, but as the locomotives are still in the new LNER livery it is probably not long after the grouping in 1923 and long before his grandson was born!

The day would start early, sometimes 4.00a.m. His engines were 'common user' engines only in BR days – before that he was responsible for his own engine, and as can be seen they were immaculately kept. His roster would be handed to him, as to all Eastern drivers, at the beginning of the shift, so he did not always know what trains he would be taking – passenger, stopping trains or freight, nor what time he would finish in the evenings.

My other grandfather, Jimmy Dennis, drove on the old Midland and Great Northern Joint Railway (MGNJR), between Yarmouth, Norwich and Melton Constable in Norfolk. It was a truly rural line, with little traffic compared to the buzz of the Great Eastern or especially the East Coast main line which had become my territory by the early 1950s.

I know relatively little about Jimmy Dennis's engines except that B12 61572, now preserved on the North Norfolk Railway, was once his regular engine. I remember well going between the factory buildings in Central Road, Cromer (where my grandparents lived at number 60) and clambering down the bank to get on the footplate of this engine as it was turned on the turntable in the yard at Cromer Beach station. The yard was always a clutter of spare parts and heaps of coal. The drivers and firemen knew where to go, but to me it was of no matter; it just represented all the sounds and smells of the steam railway that any railway enthusiast would enjoy so much.

Cromer had two stations miles apart. Cromer Beach served the town centre and was mostly used for local traffic on the MGNJR. Holiday traffic from Liverpool Street, London, and from Norwich ended up at Cromer High, which as its name implies was high above the town towards Overstrand. The High station was an early victim of cuts, before Beeching, and traffic was then sent to Cromer Beach which was and is a terminus. This entailed trains working in and out to either go back to Norwich or to Sheringham; hence the turntable. This practice still persists today although diesel multiple units do not require turning and the station is an apology of its former self. The line was singled from Roughton Road junction downgrade to Beach station. The signal box was located at the end of Jimmy Dennis's smallholding. Drivers had to collect or leave a tablet to gain single-line occupancy. The signalman in the junction box was one Mr Barton who was probably only in his early twenties when the photograph overleaf was taken. Many happy days were spent in this box, learning the bell codes and watching the diminishing number of trains passing by. The signalman had very little to do. Mr Barton had a shotgun in the signal box which he used to poach the woodpigeon and pheasant on my grandfather's land opposite.

One can wonder what the wheel set was from at the front of the box. The tablet catcher is in the foreground but the drivers never used it as it was far too easy to injure arm or hand attempting to get the iron loop which held the tablet pouch over the hook at 10 to 15mph. If Signalman Barton was not there to collect it the driver would throw it at the base of the box!

The signal box at the end of Jimmy Dennis's smallholding, taken about 1959 with the author's first camera, a Kodak Box Brownie 127.

This narrative illustrates how the enginemen were affected by their training and the particular conditions of the lines they were apprenticed to. The pressure of driving on the main lines was very different from the laid-back life on the rural ones. The drivers from Kings Cross, Camden Old Oak or any of the larger sheds had a much more varied existence and consequently had to be able to cope with that. A sight of the examination sat by an apprentice fireman to become a passed fireman on the LNER in 1933 makes our present-day GCSE examinations in mathematics, science and English look incredibly simple. Loyalty to a particular railway was very strong and very few drivers moved from one region to another, even in BR days. In any case steam only lasted for twenty years after 1948, and that was hardly enough time for a cleaner to become a lower link driver. The days of high-visibility vests and second men were a long way away.

One

The Eastern Region

The Eastern was formed from the territory of the old LNER; this in turn was formed from a myriad of smaller railways on 1 January 1923 at the time of the grouping. The main players in the LNER were the Great Northern which ran into the London termini of Kings Cross and the Great Eastern into Liverpool Street. The other London termini saw traffic from mainly these and a variety of other railway companies. Further north they in turn were linked to their northern counterparts, the North Eastern Railway and even the Great North of Scotland Railway. It was evident that all of these lines led to London, so locomotives from them occasionally found themselves in the metropolis. With the grouping and then nationalisation, it was much easier for, say, locomotives from Newcastle or Edinburgh to make the journey to Kings Cross, but in fact they seldom did so, and one of the joys of train spotting in the London area was hoping to see a locomotive that was rarely seen so far south. The working practices of engine sheds changed little from LNER to BR days, and although some sheds tended to hang on to foreign engines in good condition, most made a point of getting their favoured machines back home as quickly as possible. Even in BR days some sheds allocated specific locomotives to only one or two crews, who would regard the chosen engine as their personal property and look after it accordingly.

The Eastern was 'my' region, not only because both my grandfathers were drivers in far-off East Anglia and nearby Bishops Stortford in Hertfordshire, but because the family lived in the growing town of Hatfield, some 20 miles north of Kings Cross. It was here that the first photographs were taken with a plastic Kodak Brownie 127. The number referred to the film size which was bigger by a factor of about x2 than 35mm in format, and films came in 12 or 24 exposure lengths. The film in the late 1950s was pretty poor stuff, mostly either Kodak or Ilford. The film mostly used was Kodak Tri-x or Ilford FP3 black and white roll films, because they were available from the local chemist, Eakins and Fischer, who also did the initial development. I should have let them carry on, because I rapidly became interested in developing my own films and poor control of safelight, developer concentration, and developing time, combined with the mess and uncertainty of developing in a dish in the cupboard under the stairs, lead to either fogged films or grain the size of golfballs! Matters improved with the purchase of a Patterson developing tank, and the grain was then at least attributable to the rather coarse films – especially Tri-x. Film speed hardly mattered. The camera had a fixed shutter speed of 1/25th of a second which was just about good enough to photograph a stationary locomotive if one held the camera very steady or rested it on a fixed platform. Attempts at shooting an A4 doing 80mph southbound through Hatfield were doomed to failure.

Soon after matters improved with the purchase of a second-hand Gnome enlarger with diffuser plates instead of condenser lenses – at least it did not damage the negatives! It took nearly three years before a slightly better camera was purchased: a Ferrania Ibis 44. It too used 127 film but had a curious 4cm square format, and consequently provided more shots for your money. More importantly it had a reasonable lens compared to the plastic bubble on the front of the Kodak, and a top shutter speed of 1/150th second. Slow-moving trains were now within my grasp.

Thus equipped I accrued some 1,000 negatives, many of which are quite useless, but some of which are of real historical interest. The majority of the photographs are of course around Hatfield and Welwyn Garden City, and I apologise for the preponderance of pictures taken in the same locations, but a bicycle was the only means of transport to reach such exotic locations such as St Albans or Harpenden until old enough to venture up to the Big Smoke. That I did so at the age of fourteen shows how time has changed. There was little risk in those days to children travelling on their own, and of course I found gangs of like-minded spotters, complete with school caps and Ian Allen's combined ABCs (ten shillings and sixpence was a fortune). Maybe you were one of them.

N7 69603 at Stratford, June 1959.

Opposite from top
Designed by G.E. Hill in 1926, the N7 0-6-2T locomotives were intended for suburban traffic, but they were such useful locomotives they sometimes found themselves on other duties such as short-haul freight, banking and shunting. N7/5 number 69654 was rebuilt in 1943. It is seen here in Hatfield yard on a murky November day in 1958. The island or northbound platform can be seen behind the engine, and the small brick-built engine shed which was allocated shed code 34C was to the left of the picture.

Preserved member of the class N7/3 69621 at Weybourne on the North Norfolk Railway in 2009. Note the Westinghouse brake for use on the Great Eastern Railway section of the Eastern region.

N2/2 shunts coal trucks in Hatfield yard in March 1959. The engine shed is discernible in the top right of the picture as is a lamp not long converted from gas. Hatfield yard was nearly always full of coal wagons, as the shed was used as a holding stage for Kings Cross.

The earlier 1925 N2 was designed by Nigel Gresley as a suburban passenger tank locomotive which could also work on the space-restricted lines around Moorgate. It was classified as 3P2F (3 passenger, 2 freight), compared to the 3MT (mixed traffic) classification of the N7. This was entirely due to the much larger 5ft 8in-diameter wheels of the N2 which made them fast running machines. The author timed one at 68mph on a London suburban working to Hatfield, but even more impressive than the maximum speed was the rapid acceleration up the bank to Holloway. The N2s would quite often work from Kings Cross to Hertford East, Cuffley, or other lines on the Great Eastern section, or more frequently from Broad Street which was immediately adjacent to Liverpool Street. Alas Broad Street station no longer exists but thankfully one of the N2s has been preserved. Like the example above, the preserved engine has the cut down chimney of a locomotive allowed to work on the Metropolitan Underground line. Chimneys so often define the 'character' of a locomotive and the squat chimney on the N2 gives it a compact and powerful appearance when compared with the N7.

The condenser apparatus on the N2 tank engines enabled them to work on the cut and cover Underground lines, following the Victorian specification that a locomotive working therein 'must consume its own smoke'! The picture above shows the preserved member of the class near Kelling on the North Norfolk Railway.

The humble tank locomotives received little attention compared to the larger locomotives on the former LNER. Probably the first thought most readers have when they think of the Eastern region is of an image of Sir Nigel Gresley's superb Pacific locomotives racing up the East Coast main line. In fact these machines were but a small part of the railway, but the publicity received by *Mallard* and the other thirty-three (originally thirty-four) members of the A4 class ensure that high-speed trains of this line will always be in the forefront of one's memories.

In the autumn of 1959 60014 *Silver Link* enters Kings Cross with a morning arrival.

The same locomotive bursts under the Hertford Road bridge between Hatfield and Welwyn Garden City in the spring of 1961. This was a panned shot as the locomotive was doing at least 80mph at this point.

Another shot panned for the same reason, and I failed to get the back end of the train in, but the spectacularly stormy cloud highlighted the white exhaust as 60029 *Woodcock* races past the outskirts of Hatfield for Kings Cross in June 1962.

1962 was the last year the A4s saw regular use on the main line in the London area, and on a summer's evening in August of that year 60025 *Falcon* heads north from Hatfield with a Leeds express. From the absence of exhaust, the engine seems to be in better internal condition than its grimy exterior indicates. Coaching stock from a southbound train can be seen under the bridge in Hatfield yard.

Facing in the opposite direction from the previous shot, and on the same evening, A4 60017 *Silver Fox* roars under the Hertford Road bridge travelling very fast on a London-bound express. The fox emblem can just be made out on the side of the boiler.

60007 *Sir Nigel Gresley* before preservation south of Welwyn Garden City, with a fine exhaust in the cold morning air of February 1962.

Forty-five years later, and resplendent in British Railways blue livery, the same locomotive enters Levisham station on the North Yorkshire Moors Railway.

Still on the East Coast line into London, 60009 *Union of South Africa* approaches the Tay Bridge in 1986 with the *Bon Accord*.

The A3 class locomotives were derivatives of H.N. Gresley's original A1 class introduced to the Great Northern Railway in 1922. In their original form there was some similarity in appearance to the Ivatt 'Atlantics' which Gresley had modified extensively with a larger boiler. The new Pacific engines were not therefore the radical departure from locomotive practice on the East Coast route that most authors seem to think. The modifications which followed showed how open-minded their designer was; he recognised the benefits of increased valve lap after the trials with a Castle class locomotive from Swindon, and promptly altered the A1s to great effect. The author has never heard of Swindon making any alterations to the Castle as a result of this trial. Perhaps Swindon's products were perfect (as most GWR supporters believe).

The modifications with a higher pressure boiler – now 220psi – and especially the banjo dome and cut down chimney, gave the locomotive a very powerful and purposeful look. It is in this form that they spent most of their lives.

An unidentified A3 with a badly burnt smokebox door northbound through Hatfeld in August 1959. Note the blood and custard-mixed livery. The bay on the left of the platform was built to accommodate the Royal Train for visits to Hatfield House.

Opposite below For a short while the A3s ran modified with a double chimney but without smoke deflectors. Here 60044 *Melton* rounds the curve south of Welwyn Garden City with an evening express in March 1962. The double chimney is said by P.N. Townsend of top shed to have given the A3s a new lease of life, and that they were then as good as the A4s. It is surprising that this had not been done earlier as Gresley was fully aware of the benefits of the double chimney from experiments with number 2751, *Humorist*. He was also aware that the double chimney gave a problem with its soft exhaust, and required some form of smoke deflection. Maybe spoiling the graceful lines of the A3 Pacifics was a step too far for this great designer.

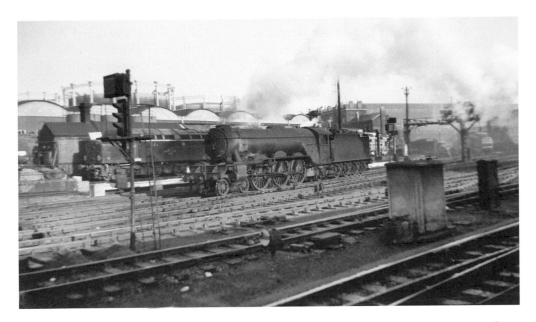

Transition from steam to diesel at the 'Cross'. The prototype Deltic can be seen peeking behind the A3's tender. This is a rare shot as not many photographs exist of the prototype machine in its blue and white livery. The A3 is also unusual in that it has the small wing-type smoke deflectors either side of the double chimney – an early and short-lived attempt to deflect the smoke upwards from the softer exhaust of these double-chimney machines.

This was the consequence of adding the double chimney, which was done in 1959. 60062 *Minoru* is on a stopping train to Peterborough on a glorious summer's evening in 1962. The drifting smoke problem was solved by those hideous elephant's ears which had only been added the same year. (German-type smoke deflectors looked fine on German locomotives!) This was a menial task for such a powerful and recently modified engine, so it may have been a running in turn. Note the Gresley carriage immediately behind the locomotive. *Minoru* was unusual, having been at various times on the Scottish region and the Great Central line, during the course of which it was changed to right-hand drive. The absence of exhaust is an indication both of the warmth of the evening and the state of health of the locomotive.

Opposite from top
60044 again, now with ears, just north of Welwyn Garden City in August 1962.

Twilight of the A3s. A down express between Hatfield and Welwyn in 1963 hauled by 60047 *Donovan*, the last year of regular steam working south of Peterborough.

Still a line into London, the most famous of all the A3 locomotives – perhaps *the* most famous locomotive ever – *Flying Scotsman* is pausing at Salisbury, this time as a preserved locomotive. Salisbury is on the old London and South Western main line into London, so *Scotsman* is a long way from its Eastern region home. It is seen here just before it too was modified with a double chimney and smoke deflectors, which spoiled its appearance completely and rendered the apple green livery totally inaccurate. Unfortunately the new 'owners', the National Railway Museum, have elected to maintain this combination.

At the time of writing this locomotive, the only member of its class to be saved, is still undergoing restoration work in the museum; it has taken over three years and cost over £3 million. One has to ask why? It appears that a brand new locomotive, an A1 called *Tornado*, was built for less…

Following the success of the A3 and A4 class locomotives, Nigel Gresley set about providing the LNER with powerful and capable mixed-traffic locomotives. These were actually slightly too large and consequently unable to run on the Great Eastern section where they would have been very useful machines on the Liverpool Street to Norwich expresses. They were given the classification V2 and were power classified as 7P6F. When modified with outside steam pipes it was difficult to distinguish a V2 from an A3 at a distance.

Opposite from top
Prototype V2 60800, named *Green Arrow* after the freight service it was designed to operate, passes under the Hertford Road bridge near Hatfield and Welwyn Garden City.

An immaculate V2 panned as it passes an early liveried diesel at Red Hall in the summer of 1959.

Between the Great North Road bridge and the Hertford Road bridge was a favourite location, as the reader will have observed. On a clear summer's evening in 1963, 60847 *St Peters School, York AD 627* heads north with a short fitted freight. This engine was one of the very few named V2s of which there were six out of a total 184 locomotives. It is interesting to note that in the Ian Allan ABCs numbers 60800 to 60872 were left with space for names to be added. Perhaps that was the intention; alas it never happened.

Only one engine of this class has been preserved, and that is 60800, *Green Arrow*, the prototype locomotive. In a way it is a pity this engine was chosen as it had the original monobloc casting for all three cylinders and inside steam pipes, unlike 60847 above. The monobloc castings are large and complex, and when they crack, as has happened to *Green Arrow*, repair is at best expensive and sometimes impossible. That is the fate of *Green Arrow*, as decided by the National Railway Museum, and after years of hauling main line steam specials resplendent in apple green livery, it is to be stuffed and mounted in the museum or maybe one of its satellite sites.

Opposite A double-chimney V2 running light on the suburban line to Welwyn Garden City in 1963. The V2s were also greatly improved in terms of efficiency (but not appearance) with the Kylchap exhaust; they never received elephant's ears. The improvement was just too late and the diesels were coming. The photograph of 60853 was taken at the same location by turning round.

1959, and an unusually clean B1 heads towards Cambridge on the suburban line. Note the Gresley coach still in use behind the tender.

Cambridge Buffet Express, accurately known as the 'beer train' to Cambridge under-graduates, learning to drink alcohol as well – one hopes – as they were learning their chosen subjects! Photographed south of Welwyn Garden City, March 1960.

61379 *Mayflower*, panned at speed, light engine at Hatfield in June 1960.

A different, preserved B1, given the same nameplate, on the Nene Valley Railway which would have connected to the Eastern region and London at Peterborough.

A1 number 60135 *Madge Wildfire* was not a common sight around the London area. It was a Darlington-built machine and suffered from the usual differences between Doncaster and Darlington as to how the valve gear should be set up. The locomotive is in a passably clean state and was running very freely when this photograph was taken of it rounding the curve near Welwyn Garden City in the summer of 1961.

The A1s as a class were very powerful machines and had the potential of being as fast as any locomotive on the main line system; however, it has been reported many times that they were rough riding. Mr Townsend of top shed should know. Under his instructions, modifications were carried out to my favourite member of this class, 60136 *Alcazar*. This included modifications to the bogie truck under the cab, allowing more side play, in a manner similar to the design of the extremely good riding A4 Pacifics. *Alcazar* always seemed to come through Hatfield a great deal faster than the other Pacifics of this class.

A completely new locomotive named *Tornado* has been constructed in 2010, and this incorporates improved suspension of the trailing bogie. I hope it rides like *Alcazar*, although it is unlikely to be allowed to get near the 100mph mark.

Madge Wildfire had only fifteen months left to run anywhere after this photograph was taken, being withdrawn in November 1962.

Opposite from top
Preserved B1 61264 passing East Runton on the Cromer Sheringham branch. This train originated in London and ran via Norwich to Sheringham.

The same locomotive in 2006 in Glenfinnan, Scotland; a long way from the East Coast main line, but connected to it via Fort William and hence Edinburgh, although this engine travelled up the West Coast!

Opposite top 60113 was nominally at least an A1. It was actually a rebuild from Nigel Gresley's original A1 Pacific *Great Northern* and is seen by most writers as an act of malice by its designer Edward Thompson against his former employer. The engine is seen here at speed on the ECML. In spite of the author's dislike for this ugly hybrid, it was a very powerful machine, but was rarely used for main line duties if an A1 or an A4 were available. This was not due to limitations of power but more likely due to maintenance problems and a tendency to cracked frames. Thompson's obsession about divided drive, and the consequent rearward location of the cylinders, lead to undue stress on the front end which was also prone to hunt from side to side at speed.

60130 *Kestrel* was the first A1 built at Darlington in 1948. The name *Kestrel* was originally carried by A4 number 4485 but the name became available when this locomotive was renamed *Miles Beevor* after one of the LNER directors.

The A1 is seen here north of Hatfield in 1962. There is an unusual amount of black smoke but the safety valves are lifting, which suggests that the driver had followed the fairly common practice of loading the firebox while in Kings Cross and sat down for the first 40 miles. This was a sensible move with an engine prone to giving sudden sideways lurches – they helped level the fire out with no effort required from the fireman. Furthermore the A1s were very good steamers, with a huge 50-square-foot grate, and could therefore be treated in this manner, whereas an A4 most definitely could not.

Kestrel was withdrawn in October 1965, one of the very last survivors of the class.

A2/3 60514 *Chamossaire* was a little more elegant, with straight-edged smoke deflectors. It is seen here heading south near Welwyn in 1960.

Gavin Morrison in his book about the A2s claimed that *Chamossaire* was the most camera shy of all the A2s, so two photographs of the same locomotive might help redress that. The locomotive still carries its original chimney which was unique among the class, as it passes south of Red Hall in the summer of 1962, running light engine.

The state of cleanliness of the machine is puzzling as this engine was in a tatty state earlier in May of the same year, as is evident in other photographs, even though it was a New England engine. New England (unlike Gateshead) had a reputation for keeping their locomotives clean, if not quite as immaculate as Kings Cross and Haymarket.

60514 was withdrawn in December 1962 and cut up for scrap in June 1963.

Opposite from top
J15 0-6-0s were a common sight on the Great Eastern section of the Eastern region, and the author photographed them in various locations such as Cromer and Bishops Stortford in Hertfordshire, both on the Liverpool Street line, if in a tortuous way! This shot of a preserved J15 in or near Weybourne on the North Norfolk Railway taken in 2010 is of better quality than the earlier ones taken on my Box Brownie in 1958.

A J15 in LNER livery, and with stovepipe chimney, passes Sheringham golf course on the North Norfolk Railway.

An unknown K3 passes through Bishops Stortford in the spring of 1958. Bishop Stortford South box can just be seen. My grandparents lived at the top of the hill, behind the beautiful lamp.

Taken almost exactly twenty-five years later, the North Norfolk Railway is in its infancy, as two preserved Eastern locomotives, saddle tank 1982 at the front and the preserved J15 behind, shunt at Weybourne, which, at the time, was the end of the line.

Relatively few Eastern region locomotives were saved from the scrap yard. Fortunately Class K2 2005, now preserved, runs on the North Yorkshire Moors line. This was once connected to London via Malton and York; now a detour is necessary via Middlesborough.

The same locomotive passes Ellerbeck Bridge on the way to Pickering.

Standard class 4 76079 leaves Grosmont on the NYMR for the engine shed which lies beyond the tunnel. Built by George Stephenson, it was one of the first railway tunnels ever built, and is only just big enough for the steam engine about to pass through it.

A southern engine on Eastern metals! Schools class locomotive *Repton* at Thomasson's Fosse.

A Midland engine in the same location. Black 5 45407 crosses the Fosse in 2006.

Standard class 4 tank 80135 at least has claim to be on its own territory, seen here at Levisham.

But some engines definitely do not belong! GWR 6619 has struggled all the way up the bank to Goathland and illustrates how the engineers designed machines for their own particular territories. These small tank locomotives were ideally suited to local passenger trains in the flatlands of the London suburbs.

Further south on the former Midland and Great Northern Joint line former Newcastle pilot engine J72 69023 in GNR livery but with a latter-day BR crest (how about that for mixing up the history) waits patiently at Sheringham for its next turn. The year is 1983.

J52 68846 is even further from home and on foreign metals at Cranmore, Somerset. It is wearing BR livery on a preserved line. Ironically, later in this book we see the same engine in GNR livery, running on the ECML in BR days!

At the end of the line from Whitby, Pickering and Malton is the city of York, now the home of the National Railway Museum with its massive display of railway artefacts from all over the world. Ex-GNR locomotive *Stirling* single number 1 (!) can just be seen on the turntable.

York was always a smart and tidy station, retaining its elegance before and after the steam era.

Further south, nearer London, Hatfield was never smart or tidy; it was the epitome of a working-class station, and was reduced to a bus shelter after steam ended. 60024 *Kingfisher*, a rare visitor to London, rushes north.

Two L1 tanks head to head in Bishops Stortford yard, 1958.

An unknown L1 arrives at Hatfield in 1958 with a Kings Cross to Hitchin local. Both scenes above featuring the L1 are unrecognisable today. The yards and sheds have in each case been demolished and the tracks removed. Hatfield resembles a bus shelter in appearance.

L1 67749 goes back to the depot after bringing a local into the 'cross, March 1959. Notice the early green-liveried type 4 behind the L1, and the shadow of the author with his Box Brownie!

Out of breath by Welwyn Garden City! The L1s were the largest 2-6-4T tank locomotives on BR and supposedly the most powerful, but they were woefully under-boiled and poor steamers.

A sequence of pictures taken in the 1980s. This one shows a type 47 with mark 2 stock, south of Hitchin. The catenary had only just been extended to north of the station, as shown below.

A HST set passes through Hitchin station. Note the fashion in coats… and in railway livery!

Turning round from the previous picture shows a northbound Deltic. The high-pitched snarl of these machines was quite unmistakable.

This view of a Deltic was taken south of Hitchin in somewhat better weather, along with the rare visitor to the line shown below.

A class 37 at the same location, with mark 1 stock.

The wires had not got as far as Sandy when this was taken, but it was nearly the end for the Deltics. Their reign as the premier motive power on the ECML was short, soon to be replaced by the intercity HST sets. The end of the Deltics seemed to spell the end of 'real' carriage compartments and quad art sets seemed light years away.

This picture is of historical interest. I was unaware of the special and also the fact that J52 1247 had been preserved in GNR livery until it came past. Note the railway enthusiasts of the day dressed in sports jackets and ties.

Even further back in time this shot was taken about 1910 or earlier, over 100 years ago. An unidentified Great Eastern Railway 2-4-2 tank locomotive poses in the yard at Bishops Stortford, with very young fireman Ernest Henry Thatcher standing on the footplate.

WD 2-8-0 90074 in a surprisingly clean condition heads south from Welwyn with a train of empty coal wagons on an early spring morning in 1962.

In sharp contrast, Hatfield yard is full and busy in the winter of 1958.

Yet another WD trundles through Hatfield station heading south with a full coal train. The locomotive still has a very full tender; the WDs were not the prettiest locomotives but they were quite efficient at the low speeds for which they were designed.

North of Hatfield on a spring morning in 1962, a WD heads for Peterborough.

90255 was making good speed on the semi-fast line near the Hertford Road when this picture was taken in 1963. Steam did not have long to go on the ECML, but the WD was steam tight, and once again with a good load of coal in the tender.

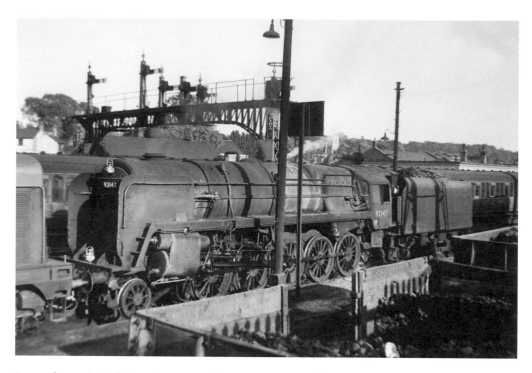

Soon the roll of the WDs was to be overtaken by the much more efficient and more powerful 9Fs. Here number 92147 in light steam waits in Hatfield yard in the summer of 1959. The yard's N2 and N7 tanks already faced competition as can be seen in front of the 9F.

On a wet November morning in 1958, 92149 passes through Hatfield heading south from Peterborough. Note the little figure on the bridge above the locomotive. That could have been me, except I was behind the camera on the platform – it cost me 2*d* for a platform ticket! All the 'infrastructure' (jargon for surrounding architecture) has long gone.

The 9Fs had a very good turn of speed as can be seen in this picture of a fitted freight on the main line heading north from Welwyn Garden City. The track was restricted through Welwyn Tunnel just to the north of this location and trains needed to clear the bottleneck quickly; in 1960 a train every 3 minutes was typical on a summer Saturday. These locomotives were sometimes used for express passenger working by Kings Cross until someone in authority calculated that the coupling rods on their ten small wheels were going round at 80mph and limited them to a top speed of 60mph!

61672
West Ham United at Stratford, 15 March 1958.

On the GE main line B1 61372 leaves a gloomy Liverpool Street station in November 1958. The carriages are still in BR blood and custard livery.

Almost exactly one year later, a grimy Britannia, 70012 *John of Gaunt*, stands in the bay of Liverpool Street station awaiting the turntable at the end of the platform.

Right Britannia class locomotive 70010 *Owen Glendower* on the ECML. It has a badly leaking right-hand cylinder but is still making good progress on a Cambridge Buffet Express. This engine spent most of its life on the GE out of Liverpool Street, but its transfer to the GNR was the beginning of the end.

Below This has to be my definitive memory of Liverpool Street station. Even on the brightest summer's day the station was gloomy and full of smoke. On a winter's day in 1958, 70002 *Geoffrey Chaucer* stands on the turntable in preparation for the 'Hook Continental' boat train from Harwich. Freshly coaled and in a reasonably clean condition (Stratford shed were proud of their Britannias), the driver stands in front of the engine while it is turned. The reader should compare this view of Liverpool Street with the modern station shown at the end of the book.

Two

The Midland Region

The Midland Region of British Railways was formed from the former LMS and operated over a wider area of the country than any other region, serving as it did the Midlands and the industrial north-west. The Midland competed fiercely with the Eastern region for traffic to Scotland, its main route being the former LNWR line from Euston to Glasgow via Shap and Beattock. The Midland also fought the Eastern most successfully for territory in the Midlands, with traffic from St Pancras to Nottingham and Derby easily outstripping the competitive efforts from Marylebone.

Their battle with the Great Western (it was never considered to be the Western region by its staff!) was less successful except in the traffic for London from Birmingham New Street where the service was quicker and more frequent than that of the GWR from Snow Hill.

So the Midland region dominated the Midlands, as its name might suggest, and it therefore had the lion's share of industrial traffic when the region was formed in 1948. Unfortunately, it failed to hang on to this, the most profitable part of any railway business in every area except the Southern. There were a number of factors in this which the author has studied over the years. Undoubtedly the convenience of road traffic, giving door to door service, played a large part in the decline of freight traffic, especially from the high densities of population in the Midlands and north-west. But the reluctance to accept freightliner containerised traffic with load-on load-off facilities by the rail unions was a major contributor to the decline, and this coupled with the Beeching report, at the instigation of Ernest Marples (who also had interests in Tarmac), accelerated the decline.

There were other contributory causes as well. The author notices a definite pattern in the care and maintenance of the steam locomotives throughout the UK.

Areas of high industrial output were generally the poorest at maintaining their steam locomotives. Thus engines from Gateshead were invariably scruffy and ill-kempt, those from Manchester on the other side of the Pennines ran Gateshead a close second, and Polmadie or St Margarets (Glasgow) did not show a particular affinity for cleaning. At the other end of the scale were engine sheds famed for their high maintenance standards; Edinburgh Haymarket, Kings Cross, Worcester, Old Oak Common, Eastleigh – none of which were in the industrial Midland region. The Midland seem to put much greater emphasis on the need for ease of maintenance than the other regions who were often fiercely loyal to the designer of their particular locomotives. So it was that the steam engine declined, and in their final years were often seen in an appalling state.

Royal Scot class 46108 *Seaforth Highlander* stands on the departure side of the old Euston in 1959. For a long time this platform was made of wood. The roof of the building was never covered as elegantly as that of Paddington (Brunel's architecture was a cut above the rest!) but at least it looked like a railway station and not a bus terminal. There were always odd trucks parked in the adjacent bay which gave the whole place a somewhat tatty appearance. The locomotive was in an unusually clean condition for the Midland and looked splendid in Brunswick green. Surprisingly this engine was rebuilt from its Fowler design during the war years in August 1943, and emerged from Crewe with a Stanier taper boiler and double chimney. In this condition the 'Scots' were powerful locomotives, but had a reputation for rough riding. *Seaforth Highlander* was withdrawn and broken up in January 1963.

The arrival of diesels made little difference to the decline, given the other problems; and it is only now, in the twenty-first century, that the destruction of the rail network has been halted.

For all of the above reasons, the author did not follow the pilgrimages to Rose Grove and the final death throes of steam, and so has relatively few shots taken of this region's fine locomotives except in preservation. I still prefer to remember Euston as it was rather than the present-day bus terminal; the Doric arch rather than the polished floor of the concourse. There is no sense of grandeur in today's departures from London, and nowhere is this loss more acute than from Euston and St Pancras, the two most radically modernised termini.

By the summer of 1960 many of Stanier's magnificent 'Duchesses' had been repainted in LMS crimson lake, in an attempt to brighten up the railway's image and reintroduce some competitive pride in the region. Titled trains became popular again – they always were on the Eastern. It was a master stroke, but too late. 46248 *City of Leeds* departs Euston with the Caledonian to Glasgow.

46239 *City of Chester* in green livery was equally well cleaned as it departs with the same train a few weeks later. The absence of train spotters on this platform was unusual!

Destined for fame if not fortune, 46229 *Duchess of Hamilton* was sent to the USA disguised as 46220 *Coronation*. It awaits departure from Euston in the early 1960s. This locomotive is now preserved and has put in some phenomenal performances on the main line since its restoration. It is currently in the National Railway Museum in its original streamlined form.

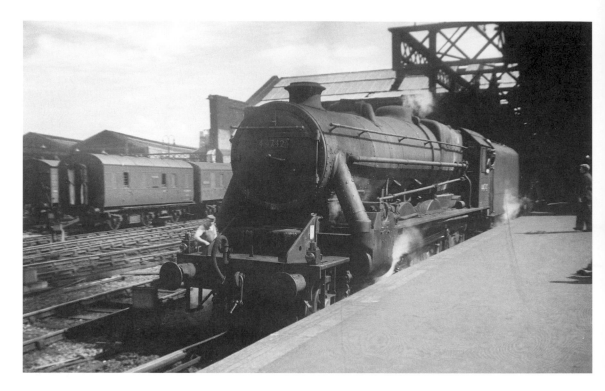

Later on in the day the sun came out and I obtained this picture of the last member of the 'Patriot' class number 45551, unmodified and un-named, backing into the station. This picture epitomises all that was exciting about the railway operation of the time; one never knew what was going to come down the hill next.

Opposite from top
Caprotti class 5 44742 awaits departure after the Caledonian shown on the previous page. These ugly ducklings were one of many attempts to improve the performance of Stanier's most successful design, the Black 5. None of the modified machines showed much improvement with the exception of 44767, the sole example equipped with Stephenson's link motion and Timken roller bearings.

Royal Scot 46157 *The Royal Artilleryman* enters Euston in 1959. A Princess Royal class locomotive can be identified by its long boiler on the departure side. Train spotters can be seen in their school uniforms everywhere!

We leave Euston on a murky winter's day in 1961 with one of William Stanier's least successful designs, a very rundown 'Jubilee' 45638 *Zanzibar* waiting at the same point. The previous member of the class, 45637, was destroyed in the Harrow and Wealdstone disaster on 8 October 1952. In the haze just visible at the rear end of a Stanier tender – probably a Black 5 – is a diesel shunter. The driver of *Zanzibar* is discussing his route with an inspector. The fireman expects to use a lot of coal on the journey: how did he get THAT under the loading gauge?

1 A preserved example of the N2 seen operating as a visitor on the North Norfolk Railway in the spring of 2010. Number 1744 is painted in GNR apple green and is complete with a beautifully restored quad-art set of teak coaches. These were designed specifically for the crowded London suburban traffic and enabled a weight reduction and shorter trainsets since the carriages each share a bogey with the next carriage. They were reputed to be very cramped and rough riding compared to Gresley's other superbly smooth-running coaches. The locomotive carries the fictitious destination board of Cuffley in Hertfordshire, showing that it would have taken the Hertford branch, probably from Liverpool Street, although Hertford could still be reached from Hatfield in the 1950s.

2 A preserved J15 taken in 2010 in or near Weybourne on the North Norfolk Railway.

3 828 and 777 *Sir Lamiel* tear under the road bridge near Petersfield towards London.

4 Heading towards Paddington, 6024 at Twerton near Bath on a still autumn morning in 2007.

5 B1 61264 leaves Cromer for Sheringham then London in May 2006.

6 At Culham, only a few miles from Oxford and heading towards Paddington, *Clan Line* is already doing 75mph with twelve coaches and a dead diesel at the rear in April 2007.

7 This special followed a circuitous route on the old Berks and will return to Waterloo much later in the evening with Standard Class 4 76079 at Stockton in the Wylye Valley in July 2007.

8 6233 *Duchess of Sutherland* heads towards London at Rodbourne in September 2007.

9 The final run of *Bradley Manor* seen leaving the Severn Tunnel at Pilning in March 2007.

10 *King Edward I* and *Earl Bathurst* on the *Great Britain* near Bridgewater in 2007. The *Great Britain* started from London and ended there after travelling the entire length of the British Isles from Penzance to the far north of Scotland using several different locomotives.

11 Having originated from Paddington yet again, 6201 *Princess Elizabeth* leaves Taunton for the South Devon banks, 2006.

12 One of the few main line tours which did not originate in London, 45407 again on the 'Scarborough Express' near Kirby, on its way to York.

13 The Torbay expresses from Bristol to Kingswear were the other regular main line excursions not to originate from the metropolis. 5029 *Nunney Castle* in Bristol Temple Meads station.

14 6233 *Duchess of Sutherland* enters Salisbury with the *Cuneo Centennial* in 2006.

15 Mickey Mouse 46521 and Standard tank 80079 leave Morton-in-Marsh for Oxford and Marylebone.

16 It was not very often that a southern engine got as far as Paddington even though there was some exchange at Oxford. In 2007 a foreigner approaches Didcot from Paddington: 35028 *Clan Line*. Note that the Western region has resisted the need for overhead electrification.

The winter of 1963 was one of the hardest on record and the railways, along with every other form of transport, struggled to keep running. Fowler tank 42335 moves empty stock out of the old St Pancras, when the station looked like a station and not a shopping arcade. Remains of the snow still lay on the platform in March, and the freezing conditions reveal every leak of steam from the 1927-built machine. Never very popular with the engine crew, they were poor steamers and lacked power. 42335 was one of the class without even a side window in the cab, which did not make shunting any easier!

Deely/Fowler 4F 43971 stand at Kentish Town. Built in 1911, these locomotives suffered problems with bearings, as did many of the Derby-designed locomotives, due to inadequate lubrication. This had less impact on the slow-moving 0-6-0s than on the compound 4-4-0s which suffered the same problem.

The elegant lines of a Black 5 number 45342 at St Albans in the spring of 1960.

The unique Stephenson's link Black 5 on the North Norfolk Railway in July 2010.

Most of the Black 5 locomotives were equipped with Walschaerts valve gear. With two outside cylinders, it was relatively easy to maintain and clean, and so the only conceivable reason for altering it was to attempt greater coal efficiency or more power. Several different gearing systems were tried. The use of Caprotti valve gear was ineffective and resulted in a very ugly machine. Stephenson's link, however, proved to be both effective and easy to maintain. Alas, the experiment was too late...

Jubilee 45628 *Somaliland* pauses at St Albans with a semi-fast to St Pancras in 1960. The Jubilees always looked less sturdy than the Black 5s, perhaps due to the extent of the taper of their boiler.

Opposite from top
An 8F simmers gently to the south of St Albans station. A railway worker seems to be trying to turn back the tide, shovelling the ash out from between the tracks with a little encouragement from the driver of the locomotive no doubt. Taken in July 1959, all the tracks and the buildings have long vanished.

From the other side of the station and on the same day, a work-stained Fairburn 2-6-4 tank waits with a train presumably from St Pancras, although it is well away from the normal running lines.

An unidentified Jubilee passes the suburbs of Harpenden on a spring evening in 1959. The running lines of the Midland were arranged totally differently from the Eastern and express trains travelled on the outer lines instead of the inner.

Long before the Midland region was formed, this group of volunteer women ran the Midland Railway at Keighley in Yorkshire during the First World War.

As steam declined preservationists started saving locomotives from the scrap yard. Carnforth on the WCML was one of the earliest preservation sites; Black 5 newly restored was one of the first…

… while much smaller engines such as the ever popular 'Jinty' tank locomotives found their way to the Great Central Railway.

Princess Royal class locomotive 46203 *Princess Margaret Rose* waits with the southbound Cumbrian Mountain Express at Carlisle, another station which has lost its elegant structure.

A V2 at Neasden in 1958.

Three

Preserved Steam on the Main Line

Many of the steam locomotives from British Railways days were withdrawn and cut up 'at a stroke'. The majority of withdrawals took place in 1962 and 1963, especially on the Eastern region, and in 1964 on the Great Western. Curiously, main line steam held on the longest on the Southern, with most of the withdrawals taking place in 1966 and 1967. More Bulleid Pacific locomotives were rescued and restored than any other class.

The end of steam came in 1968 with the very last steam locomotives operating out of Rose Grove. The infamous 15-guinea special was British Railways' official final passenger steam train; although steam lingered on a few weeks in industrial areas, it was officially banned from the main line.

The ban was probably the biggest publicity error BR could have made. As soon as people are told they cannot have something, they want it! The resistance to steam was probably greatest at York, and it is ironical that the National Railway Museum should be adjacent to York Station.

The next section is a record of some of the achievements of the volunteers, paid and unpaid, who have kept steam running on the main line. The pictures cover all regions. All the (remaining) lines into London have now seen preserved steam. In fact one of the benefits of the relaxation of the steam ban was that locomotives could run on lines previously not open to them, so we have been able to compare the performance of Eastern region Pacifics on Shap and Midland region engines on the Devon banks. Sometimes all has gone well, sometimes not. The author has travelled on too many trips which have not been steam hauled because of locomotive failure. Nonetheless the sight and sound of steam running at speed on the main line is still one of the most wonderful forms of entertainment to so many.

Above Princess Margaret Rose climbs Horsfield Bank out of Bristol.

Opposite from top
Well removed from London and its smoke-free zone, Black 5 5407 at Carnforth during the steam ban.

With a special that started from Paddington, the pioneer 'Britannia' number 70000 leaves Didcot for Oxford in the 1990s.

Having left Waterloo and travelled to Southampton via Eastleigh, 34067 *Tangmere* was photographed on the Royal Wessex in the Wylye Valley in 2007.

BB nameplate photographed at Waterloo.

Four

The Southern Region

The Southern region was basically a continuity of the old Southern Railway formed by the grouping in 1922, so the region had much in common with the GWR in this respect, including resentment over disputed territory! While the Southern served the whole of the region south of the Thames, including the Kent coast, the south coast and ferry ports to the Continent, it also sought to gain control of the port of Plymouth in the South West. Here the conflict arose between the Southern and the GWR. The latter gained the ascendancy with its well-oiled publicity machine, and the route via Salisbury to Exeter and Plymouth became known as the 'withered arm'.

This part of the Southern was never electrified with the third rail electrification system used over the rest of the region by Sir Herbert Walker, and Maunsell was also a financially astute and cautious CME prior to the outbreak of hostilities. However, Oliver Bulleid, the CME for the Southern Railway from the start of the war, was a prolific, if at times somewhat eccentric, designer, and produced a large number of very unconventional Pacific locomotives for the Southern Railway. It was quite likely that Oliver Bulleid was held somewhat in check by Nigel Gresley when he served under that great engineer on the LNER. Be that as it may, released from all constraints OVS (as he was known) produced steam electric, diesel and electric locomotives as well as carriages of unconventional and conventional design. His Leader class locomotive was his biggest failure – two were built but neither ran in revenue-earning service, which is probably as well or the rail unions may have walked out en masse!

His air-smoothed Pacifics were modified by Bond in the 1950s and continued to serve the railway well right to the end of steam on the Southern in 1967. Indeed, with such an excess of steam power available, the Southern felt no need to electrify the withered arm and so prolonged the life of steam on that line.

Modified Merchant Navy class 35013 *Blue Funnel* arrives under the canopy of Waterloo in 1959, with a train from Salisbury, as denoted by the two-disc head code (number 9).

Opposite from top
Merchant Navy 35028 *Clan Line* at Gillingham on its way to Salisbury in 2006.

Lord Nelson class 30860 *Lord Hawke* waits at Waterloo with a train for Bournemouth in the summer of 1959. Note the wagon next to the tender, a typical Southern practice.

Lord Nelson number 850 in Southern Railway malachite green as preserved and running on the main line near Hanging Langford in the Wylye Valley in 2007.

M7 tank on shunting duties at Waterloo in 1960. These tank locomotives were used almost exclusively for the West of England trains at Waterloo – all other services were electrified.

A glint shot before they became fashionable! 35013 stands at the end of the platform waiting to return to Stewarts Lane. Note the gangers behind the tender: 'What 'elf and safety?'

Rebuilt Merchant Navy 35005 *Canadian Pacific* at Mitcheldever on a Southampton-bound express in 2006. Both the station and track were in a dreadful state.

C class 31510 with incorrect head code takes empty stock out of Waterloo past Vauxhall in the summer of 1960. How diminutive the driver appears, even if he is seated!

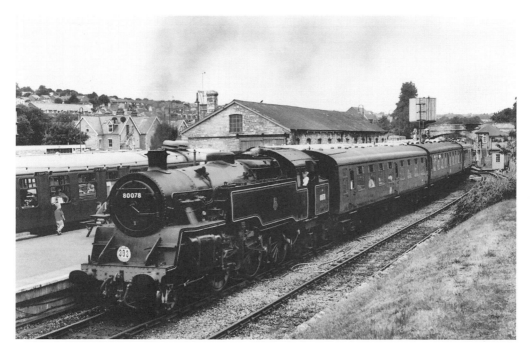

Standard class 4 as preserved at Swanage in 2007 looks too large for such a small train.

S15 class number 828, as preserved and still running on the main line, passes through Fareham on its way to Southampton in 2006. The end of the platform is crowded with photographers.

Opposite from top
King Arthur class 30777 *Sir Lamiel* passes through Grately en route to Salisbury.

Also on the 'withered arm' approaching Buckhorn Weston is standard class 5 73096 with the green train on the singled section of the line which restricts so much traffic.

Clan Line watering at Salisbury as it has on many occasions during its BR life.

B4 30096 and Schools 30923 *Bradfield* at Eastleigh in 1955.

Salisbury was a very difficult station to restart a heavy train due to its sharp curve in the eastbound direction, as can be seen here with number 828 awaiting departure.

Clan Line makes light work of the Bournemouth Belle at Grately in 2007.

The Bluebell Railway had been 100 per cent steam operated until 2009; here their standard class 5 *Camelot* departs Horstead Keynes. The SR wagons are perfectly restored.

West Country class 21C123 *Blackmore Vale* on the Bluebell Line.

32424 at
Brighton in
1950.

Both pages
A rare visitor to the Southern, even in preservation, the unique three-cylinder BR Pacific
Duke of Gloucester seen in July 2006 near Templecombe on a day of contrasting weather.

A preserved 100-year-old Southern locomotive, the E1 110 did not even make it into the 1957 Ian Allan locospotters' ABC. It is seen here on the East Somerset Railway – GWR territory.

On a stormy day in 2006 the green Standard class 5 heads west from Templecombe.

The Blackmore Vale Expresses brought crowds to Salisbury, especially when A3 *Flying Scotsman* was there on the same day as *Clan Line*.

Scotsman's external condition may look fine on the photograph, but the boiler was in a two-tone version of apple green, and the high mileages run in preservation were beginning to show.

Lord Nelson, number 850, could be heard miles away struggling up the bank at Upton Scudamore near Westbury, heading south towards Warminster in summer 2007.

Unmodified Battle of Britain *Tangmere* heads towards Southampton on a very dirty winter's day in 2007.

73096 climbs the hill out of Templecombe…

…while the old and the new stand side by side at Salisbury.

777 Sir Lamiel in early preservation days on the Severn Valley Railway.

30075 is a look-alike USA tank, seen here on the East Somerset Railway in 2004.

West Country 34105 *Swanage* at night.

Another West Country, *Blackmore Vale*, on the Bluebell Line in 2006.

Clan Line gets attention at Salisbury after bringing in the Solent and Sarum…

… while *Stepney* takes a rest from driver training on the Bluebell Line.

Small-chimney 928 *Stowe* at Cranmore en route to the Bluebell Line in the late 1980s.

Repton, also with a small chimney, waits at Grosmont on the North Yorkshire Moors line.

Battle of Britain class *Tangmere* at Lavington in 2006…

…and in 2007 in pouring rain on foreign metals passing Twerton.

Conditions were not any better for modified West Country *Taw Valley* climbing out of Bristol in 2005…

…but they were better on the Berks and Hants, near Warminster, earlier in the same year.

828 was the second steam special in the day immediately preceding another with GWR *Nunney Castle* between Westbury and Frome on the Berks and Hants line.

A4 Pacific 60009 *Union of South Africa* looks out of place on single tracks as it approaches Gillingham. It went on to make a record ascent of Whiteball on its return journey to Bristol.

A memory of the Southern. By 1963 steam was still the main source of power on trains to the West Country, and *Lord Hawke* is about to take over such a train. The Lord Nelsons were modified by O.V. Bulleid, including the strange LeMaitre exhaust system and oversized chimney.

Five

The Great Western Region

As far as God's Wonderful Railway was concerned, neither the grouping in 1922 to form the GWR nor nationalisation in 1948 changed its character or purpose. The Western always benefited from the continuity of its designs and the far-sightedness of its early CMEs, in particular Gooch and Churchward. The GWR introduced standardisation before any other railway contemplated it, with a standard range of boilers that could be swapped with other, different classes of similar power. They also used a standard frame design, standard wheels and tenders. It all gave rise to a high level of efficiency and a profitable operation, especially as the components of their steam locomotives were so advanced in concept and build quality that it took the other railways many years to catch up; for example Nigel Gresley, great engineer though he was, learnt a sharp lesson about long travel, short lap valve gear from the locomotive exchange between a castle and a brand new A1 (later A3) on the LNER. The LMS imported William Stanier from Swindon to revitalise the locomotive affairs of the Midland. OVS on the Southern did not seem to take much notice of GWR practice and as a result produced a lot of very non-standard, difficult to maintain machines.

Even British Railways learnt from advanced GWR practice, for example as an aftermath to the terrible disaster at Harrow and Wealdstone in the early 1950s. Had the GWR's track signalling system, known as ATS, been in use, that disaster could not have happened. This was a classic case of 'not invented here'. Every railway believed their own practices were best – none wanted to adopt the practices of other railways. Oh that the other lines had practiced the same level of maintenance and indeed cleanliness!

Not that the GWR got everything right. In time the LNER and the LMS, and even the all-welded boilers of the Southern Pacifics, showed engineering advances that Swindon might have benefited from. But the GWR locomotives were designed with boilers and fireboxes that suited the soft Welsh coal that was used on that line whereas the LNER and LMS used harder coals from Yorkshire and Lancashire and so had different boiler and firebox designs. Attempts by British Railways to run standard locomotives on the GWR were, at times, difficult. The BR locomotives were more closely related to Crewe than Swindon and so did not take the Welsh coal, nor the firing techniques of the GWR as well on the Western as they did elsewhere. This, coupled to a massive pride by the engine crew in anything Swindon built and a reluctance to accept anything else, meant that the GWR continued to operate with their own fleet of locomotives right to the end of steam.

Nor was the continuity only to be found in the locomotive practice. The stations were somehow always neater, tidier and cleaner than any of the other regions. As a follower of all that was LNER as a boy, I found this difficult to accept, but in hindsight it remains especially true. While Euston station was awesome, Waterloo vast, and Liverpool Street a cathedral of steam, Paddington was – and still is – all of these and clean as well! Isambard Kingdom Brunel's great designs were to be found everywhere. Bristol Temple Meads is still a beautiful station matched perhaps only by York although it has to be said the Bristol station is not Brunel's original train shed. However, it was the suburban and the country stations where the GWR excelled. Alas, with the formation of BR even here the standards slowly fell, as, it seems, the pride ebbed away. Paddington can be seen in some of the pictures with junk left about, and litter between the tracks, no different from Euston or Kings Cross. At least the copper-capped chimneys and the brasswork still shone on the Kings and Castles. There was still nowhere quite like the Western even at the end of steam.

Opposite from top
This picture typifies both Paddington and the GWR in general. Immaculate Castle class 7011 *Banbury Castle* arrives on a summer's morning in 1960.

Forty-six years later 5029 *Nunney Castle* is in an equally immaculate condition as it passes Pilning with *The Red Dragon* from South Wales to Bristol. Neither train comprises the beautiful chocolate and cream coaching stock which so distinguished the GWR.

The prototype King class locomotive 6000 *King George V* backs out of Paddington for Old Oak Common in July 1960. The engine still carries the bell presented to it during its tour of the USA where its power for such a 'small' engine greatly impressed the American engineers. They would have been even more impressed by the performance if it had been equipped at that time with the double chimney although in the author's view it slightly marred the appearance. Swindon experimented with various versions of chimney, but in the end settled for this one. Ironically the same chimney had to be cut down for operation in preservation on class mate 6024 *King Edward I* in order to clear the bridges safely, especially as track levels had been raised by a few inches as fresh ballast was frequently laid on top of old during track realignment programs. It shows how large the Kings were in relation to the loading gauge even in BR days; in fact on the grounds of their 40,000lb tractive effort the GWR claimed them to be the most powerful express locomotive in Britain at the time of their construction.

Opposite from top
King Edward I in preservation with authentic chocolate and cream coaching stock climbs Horfield bank out of Bristol Temple Meads in 2006.

At the same location a year earlier 70000 *Britannia* and a GWR mogul attempt to beat the record for the ascent of the bank! Alas signals prevented this being achieved.

Castle class 5054 *Earl of Ducie* is given the task of removing empty stock from Paddington in 1959, a job usually ascribed to the pannier tank locomotives such as 0-6-0 number 8458 shown below on the same platform in 1960.

At least the coaching stock are uniform and head code authentic on the 2006 Torbay
Express departing Bristol Temple Meads on one of the most scenic railway journeys in
the world.

And here is the same train in 2007 approaching Taunton.

At Twerton, Southern region WC *Tangmere* heads for Paddington in 2007.

Opposite from top
On a sunny summer day in 1959 *King William* arrives at Paddington possibly on a short running in turn as it still has plenty of coal left in its tender.

However, the weather was not always good and 7027 *Thornbury Castle*, although clean, does not glisten as usual. I hope 7017 *G.J. Churchward* on the left did not leave with the cable drum still on its buffer beam! There are signs of the GWR in decline.

An unidentified Castle with the original pattern double chimney heads a special towards the terminus past Old Oak Underground station in 1960.This was a great place to see all the trains in and out of Paddington, especially as westbound trains were putting steam on and just getting into their stride. Unfortunately the station staff were never very fond of train spotters cluttering up the platform and I was ejected before I could take any more photographs, a situation rather similar to that on the Southern region termini of today, although our present circumstances are very different with the advent of terrorist violence and the threat it poses to the railways.

The driver of the special has, however, seen me, and 'pipped' his whistle. I always found the drivers to be affable and even to respond to signs held up such as 'Smoke Please'!

Opposite Looking towards the concourse end of Paddington, *King Edward I* can be seen waiting with a summer Saturday express. The taller chimney as originally used by BR is evident especially when compared with the shorter one on the same locomotive in preservation below.

Hawksworths 'County' class were much more elusive than the Kings and Castles, and none have survived into preservation. They were not popular with the engine crew. They were powerful, but had very heavy coal consumption and a tender which ensured poor visibility and a draughty cab, even if it did contain more much needed coal! These were seen at Paddington in 1959 and 1960 respectively.

Prairie tank locomotive 6142 waits one evening with a local train at Paddington in 1959.

The spirit of the GWR branch line train is captured in this shot taken near Watchet on the West Somerset Railway. That line is now definitely linked to the main line at Taunton and has even handled Network Rail freight traffic on contract, and so qualifies as a line into London. The small prairie of the 4500 class, number 5542, together with its rake of chocolate and cream coaches, are in immaculate condition on a bright summer's day in 2006.

The West Somerset is also home to a number of decidedly un-Western products, none more so than Midland 8F number 88 painted in the livery (which it never previously carried) of the Somerset and Dorset. 9351 is even less authentic – it is a tank engine rebuilt.

Another Castle with the original pattern double chimney backs out of Paddington on its way back to Old Oak Common.

Nunney Castle with its single chimney waits inside Bristol Temple Meads. Only the Network Rail-style headlamp betrays the year: 2006.

No doubt about the vintage of this though: 2007 and a double-headed partnership of *King Edward I* and Castle class *Earl Bathurst* on its last main line run before its boiler ticket expired. Photographed near Dawlish.

Opposite from top
The Hall class locomotives were the equivalent of the Black 5 on the LMS. They were extremely versatile maids of all work with a good turn of speed. This one looks rather work stained at Paddington in 1960.

Two 'Halls', with 4965 *Rood Ashton Hall* at the front, near Hullavington in 2007.

This 1959 shot of a King returning to Old Oak summarises the approaching end of steam…

…and on a dirty winter's day 7020 *Gloucester Castle* stands in light steam along with a Hall and many others at Old Oak Common. It was to be the last winter of steam at the shed.

Fortunately it was far from the end of steam on Western metals. The GWR and KGV saw the end of the steam ban. Here Battle of Britain class 34067 *Tangmere* speeds past Cogload Junction, near Taunton, in 2006…

…while in 2003 Merchant Navy class *Clan Line* does the same past Frome, Somerset.

King Edward I is still a regular visitor to Bristol Temple Meads…

…although it sometimes looks out of place surrounded by high-speed trains.

With Driver Burns at the regulator, it was 10 minutes ahead of schedule at Highbridge…

…while non-GWR motive power is able to show its paces. Here *Princess Margaret Rose* passes a packed gallery at Pilning, approaching Bristol from the Severn Tunnel…

…and *Princess Elizabeth* makes a wonderful noise getting up the bank at Horsfield.

In the spring of 2006 Jubilee *Leander* plays with a load of six coaches at Newport…

...and in the summer of the same year 71000 *Duke of Gloucester* shows that Horsfield bank is just a minor bump...

...and its descent into the Severn Tunnel at 70mph is still one of the fastest on record.

This symbolises all that is Great Western: *City of Truro* at Toddington in September 2007.

In 2006 *City of Truro* ran a very special special – the centenary of its record-breaking run on the ocean mail during which the self-appointed Victorian railway expert Dr Charles Rous-Marten 'timed' the train at 100mph, although the first authentic record of 100mph goes to the LNER *Flying Scotsman*. There is little doubt though that *Truro* was close to the magic 'ton'.

In 2004 the preserved GWR mogul with a plain chimney descends Horfield bank into Bristol.

The beginning of the twenty-first century saw diesels with coupling rods. Bristol Temple Meads is the venue.

By 2009 even the future of the high-speed train units (seen here at Norton Fitzwarren) is in doubt; electrification will eventually overtake even the mighty GWR.

Six

The London Termini

All the lines in this book have a connection to London, even the preserved railways. One only has to look at the map of the railways of Britain both before and after Beeching to see that practically every line focussed on London. The 'cross-country lines' such as the Midland and Great Northern Joint, and the Cheshire Lines Committee may have been cross-country but they were just as surely linked to the capital at their termini, and depended on the capital for some of their revenue – how else did the farm produce of East Anglia get to Smithfield, or the industrial and agricultural products of Cheshire and Lancashire?

So this, the last section of the book, looks at the termini in the capital itself. The decline of the wonderful Victorian architecture and the loss of the atmosphere of the railway and the spirit of adventure it conveyed is deeply felt by many. One only has to reflect on the changes brought by the removal of the Doric arch at Euston or the building of the shopping arcade now called Liverpool Street to realise what has been lost.

Some stations have completely disappeared. It is no longer possible to photograph even the remains of London Broad Street, for example. It is wire fenced, in the process of demolition and surrounded by ultra modern high-rise office blocks. The author fondly remembers seeing N2 tank engines passing through Hatfield – usually tender first – with a destination board of 'Broad Street'.

It seems at the time of writing that every one of the London termini are in the process of 'rebuilding' to accommodate the belated resurgence of the railway as a means of transport. The role of many of these stations has changed. Instead of handling a mixture of perishable and non-perishable freight, mail and passengers, now only an ever-increasing load of passengers remain. Mass transport has arrived on a grand scale to replace the daily commute or the occasional special trip to Scotland, Cornwall, the Lakes, or even Brighton!

London has become a truly multicultural city, and has imported some of the problems of other countries too. Terrorism is a real threat as bombs explode at Euston and, terribly, at Kings Cross. The people of London and the railways withstood the Blitz in the Second World War. Such destruction and loss of life is unlikely to stop Londoners, but the operation of the stations, the freedom to walk on platforms and the vigilance of the railway staff – these have all been irrevocably changed. Barriers now guard the platforms; staff are wary of photographers; and the stations to the south of the Thames do not allow photographers on any platform unless they are travelling.

Even the Underground has seen massive changes in the last forty years; regrettably this does not include an improvement to the track or the punctuality of the inner city lines! Baker Street station, where it all began, looks much as it always has, but the ownership of the 'Tube' as it is erroneously called, has changed many times. Long gone are the electric locomotive-hauled trains to Aylesbury where one could travel in 'real' carriages, albeit eight passengers to the compartment and smokers allowed!

The Underground was built by private companies following Henry Hudson and the boom years of railway mania. The very first line to be constructed was the Metropolitan line, and the Act for it was passed by Parliament in 1854. Even in those days the activities of politicians were very often swayed by their personal interests, and some of them had invested heavily in the Great Western Railway who were actively backing the construction of the Metropolitan line between Paddington and Farringdon, thus connecting the stations of Euston, St Pancras, Kings Cross and within walking distance of Liverpool Street. The first station to be opened was Baker Street in 1863. One can still see the wide, arched roof and sufficient distance between the platforms to enable two tracks of Brunel's broad gauge to be laid.

The electric locomotives were relatively newcomers on the Underground. The first electric locomotives ran in 1890, once again a world first, but until that time steam ruled supreme even underground. The early underground trains were not truly underground, in fact most of them were above ground and so were able to enjoy the same loading gauge as their steam-hauled counterparts on the main line. These early lines were built on the 'cut and cover' principle and in 1900 over 55 per cent of the lines were above ground. That percentage has only changed in recent years with the construction of the new Victoria and Jubilee lines.

These, and the lower-level lines, the Northern, Bakerloo and Central, were all built using new boring equipment first used in the early 1900s and were able to travel under the Thames, avoiding the myriad pipes and cables beneath the surface of London. By necessity, these lines have a much smaller loading gauge; these are the real tube lines, and anyone who has travelled on them in the rush hours will confirm that is exactly what they feel like!

Bo-Bo electric Number 4 *Lord Byron* at Baker Street and Number 5 *John Hampden* at Moorgate station in 1958. Note the office block; the destruction had begun!

Metropolitan line stock (long since scrapped) at Moorgate on the same dull day.

In better weather in 1959 number 10 *W.E. Gladstone* at Baker Street. This engine survived until 1 January 1962. Four other locomotives lasted until March of that year, the last to be scrapped was, ironically, number 2 *Oliver Cromwell*.

At least the
Underground station
still exists!

The second line to open was the Hammersmith and City line in 1863, also originally broad gauge but then rapidly changed to be dual gauge as it became evident, even to the Great Western, that Stephenson's 'standard' gauge would prevail. By 1865 the GWR was losing interest in its Underground investments, to some extent because of the gauge war and the Circle line, started in 1868 and completed by 1884 was constructed to the standard gauge. This was followed in 1890 by the Northern Line then in 1900 by the Central. The Bakerloo followed in 1906.

Private building of the Underground continued until 1933 when the railways were amalgamated to form 'London Transport' in much the same way as the main lines had been amalgamated to form the big four. The Victoria line was built in 1968 and the Jubilee line in 1979. Even this did not prevent further change, and the politicians got into the act again in 1985 when Margaret Thatcher's Conservative government privatised the whole venture and called it London Underground Limited.

Sure enough, it made a profit to start with, but cuts in the staff lead to poor cleaning and reduced maintenance, poor track work and eventually the inevitable happened; a fire caused loss of life, and the whole company ethos had to be reviewed.

Today the Underground has 270 stations and 250 miles of track. It is the second largest such system in the world, and the oldest. In 2007 it carried over one billion passengers. It is in dire need of re-investment again, especially in the inner city. London Underground, I fear, will experience the same customer-driven modifications as the rest of the railway stations in London. Let us hope they are completed more sympathetically.

Kings Cross was not far behind Euston (who were calling themselves 'the Premier Line' much to the annoyance of the Great Northern Railway). These two lines into London were always destined to compete with one another for the Scottish traffic and still do to this day. There are exciting reminders of the Victorian era and these have been well documented by historians such as O.S. Nock in his book *The Railway Races to the North*. Such was the competition between the two companies, but Kings Cross was referred to as the seat of the GNR as was Euston on behalf of the London and Birmingham and later the LNWR.

Cubitt built the station on the site of an old smallpox hospital! Where it replaced the original station, a temporary terminus at Maiden Lane which was used between 1850 and 1852. The original Kings Cross station was cramped and had only two platforms. Indeed the whole area from Kings Cross eastwards towards Mount Pleasant (so called by the Victorians as it was a giant refuse disposal area and stank!) was fairly grim; it seems to have changed little in recent years, in spite of the redevelopment of the East End. Today the station looks shoddy with a tatty concourse built in 1972 but due for removal by 2012.

Opposite from top
This is the view Robert Stephenson would have from his statue outside Euston station. No doubt it would make him shudder. Euston was the first inter-city station in London. It opened to the public on 20 July 1837 and served the London and Birmingham Railway which was being engineered by the great Robert Stephenson. The directors commissioned Philip Hardwicke and Charles Fox to design and build the original station, which features in earlier pictures in this book, but the building was done by none other than William Cubitt who went on to design and build that most cubic of stations, Kings Cross! Euston, by comparison, was a masterpiece, and epitomised the grandeur of Victorian travel in its superb Doric arch which I remember well. Passing through it immediately gave a sense of importance, adventure, travel, romance, whatever you were looking for. Its destruction was official vandalism and the aims of the Doric Arch Society to get it replaced in the next rebuilding as announced by British Land in 2007 should get priority. It is too much to hope for that the Grand Hall, as designed by Hardwicke's son, could ever be restored, but it is difficult to imagine anything much more soul-less than the present-day structure.

Euston. Shopping arcade or concourse (without seats of course….)?

Euston buffer stops, August 2010. Clean, functional, modern – and devoid of character.

The Cross, as railwaymen call it, the station not much changed since the days of steam; the original roof is largely intact, and so is the somewhat grimy appearance!

A high-speed train unit stands on the west side of Kings Cross in August 2010…

…while on the east side work has started on building an extra platform – and not nine and three quarters as indicated by the luggage trolley half disappearing through a wall at the station at the moment for Harry Potter fans!

The outside of the Cross has changed little apart from the mess of the catenary. But what is the scaffolding for? The date is August 2010.

Paddington was only just behind Euston in terms of opening a station in the capital, which it did on 4 June 1838; not Brunel's magnificent train shed which opened in 1854. Brunel's designs were often more austere and plain than the end product – many other architects helped him. In the case of Paddington it should really be M. Digby Wyatt's statue that graces the platform rather than Brunel's, but since Stephenson was being associated with anything emanating from Euston, Brunel ensured his name was also being recognised at Paddington! In fact, Robert Stephenson was totally unlike his father George, or Brunel, both of whom were quite deliberate self-publicists. Once again Philip Charles Hardwicke (the son) had a hand in the design of the Great Western Hotel. How the names of these famous architects are linked to so many splendid pieces of railway architecture. The station was enlarged and a fourth span put in by the outbreak of the First Word War.

Paddington is still one of the busiest and best-looking stations in London, having suffered relatively little in the way of 'modernisation'. It has sixteen platforms and the concourse, although the area known as the lawn has become a shopping precinct as well, but not in the overpowering manner of Euston, Waterloo, Victoria or Liverpool Street. Happily, the station roof has been renovated to its original standard.

Paddington: Ancient and modern still look good together.

Looking towards the concourse in the central span of Paddington. This picture was not even taken during the rush hour, showing just how busy the station is.

The GWR's rival to the West Country was the original London and South Western Railway which was incorporated into the Southern Railway on 1 January 1923, although the proposals and agreements were all drawn up in 1922. The LSWR operated from Waterloo, a station with a very different history from Paddington. It opened on 11 July 1848 and was called Waterloo Bridge station, a bridge it would cross in due course and link up with Charing Cross. The original Waterloo station was designed by William Tite, but it expanded too rapidly and became a multiplicity of stations, each with their own booking office and using their own definition of 'railway time'! In 1899 the LSWR decided the confusion could not continue and rebuilt the station, which had become something of a slum itself. The new station took twenty-three years to complete – surely the longest railway construction work in London. It finally opened in 1922 with twenty-one platforms and one of the largest concourses in Europe. The main entrance is known as the Victory arch, and is a memorial to the Southern railwaymen killed in both wars.

The clock at the centre of the concourse became famous as a meeting place ('under the clock at Waterloo') and features in various films.

Waterloo remains one of the largest, busiest stations in Europe with 88 million people passing through the station from the Southern Railway lines alone in 2008/9. The rush hour at Waterloo is something to be avoided! The arrival and departure boards are complex, as is the network of lines outside the metropolis. Only Clapham Junction is busier than Waterloo, and that is because the lines from Victoria and Waterloo merge here, all of which were controlled at one time by a manual signal box!

Waterloo was formerly the station connected to Paris via the Eurostar terminal, the train shed of which can be seen in the centre of the following photograph behind the commuters making a dash for the barrier. It seems to the author that Waterloo was a much more logical place for Eurostar than its present location at St Pancras.

Waterloo rush hour. The original Eurostar train shed can be seen at the end of the platform.

The relocation of the Eurostar terminal may be related to the accessibility of the terminal to central London. Waterloo is south of the Thames and travellers find that any crossing of the Thames is congested at peak times. Since Waterloo is linked to Charing Cross with through lines to that station which is on the north side of the Thames, and ideally located for the City and the West End, one wonders why that station was not developed as the Eurostar terminal in the first place. Charing Cross was originally built in 1864 with an iron roof over six platforms; as was the habit at the time, a railway hotel was opened at the concourse end of the platforms (compare Euston, St Pancras, Liverpool Street, Paddington...). This was originally considered to be the official centre of London.

Following the collapse of the original roof in 1905, a new station was built and the station reopened in 1906. The station was accessed from Waterloo by the rickety Hungerford footbridge which crossed the river on the eastern side and at eyeball level with the railway, separated only by the iron lattice girders of the bridge. This was a journey the author regularly undertook, as the Royal Festival Hall is adjacent to Waterloo and at the southern end of the bridge. Charing Cross at least looked like a station then. In its modern guise, having been rebuilt along with the rickety bridge in the early 1990s, it looks like the front of an Odeon cinema, with the inevitable development of shopping arcades and offices. As for Hungerford bridge (now on the western side and affording tourists a better view of Westminster if not St Paul's), at least the rickety version had charm and, yes, romance. Now its pillars obscure the front of the station and the original iron girders do the rest. One can tell it is a station by the occasional noise of a train rumbling across the almost invisible zone behind them.

The relocated Hungerford bridge and rebuilt Charing Cross station.

Victoria station is another major station serving the south but is on the north side of the Thames and is considered to be part of Central London. It is always a source of surprise how close these termini are; the author was able to walk round a circuit which included the majority of the London termini in a day. Victoria is second only to Waterloo in its passenger volume, as can be seen from the busy concourse above.

Victoria lies to the north-west of Waterloo, and its major traffic is concentrated towards the south coast, and especially towards Gatwick Airport. The station seems to have evolved rather than having been designed! It arose because of the inability or unwillingness of Victorian gentry to walk across any of the bridges to conduct their business in Westminster or the East End! It seems to have had an opening date of around October 1860 through the offices of the London Brighton and South Coast Railway. It also seems that the GWR did their level best to oppose that opening by opposing a merger of the LBSC with another railway which then might have competed with them! In any event, the GWR became a part owner of Victoria station and did not relinquish its hold until 1932. It even installed its own broad gauge out of the station to Southall in West London, until persuaded to abandon it for the standard gauge.

Victoria, like Waterloo, handled the traffic of two world wars. Recent publications and documentary programs have revealed just how much traffic the railways did handle, much of it under great secrecy. There is a plaque commemorating the body of the unknown warrior on Platform 8. The Southern railways were fiercely patriotic (indeed the railways and their staff were everywhere), perhaps because they saw so much of the troop movements in and out of London. Victoria, like Waterloo, suffered extensively from bombing during the Second World War.

Victoria became the station to use for travelling to France after the war with the Night Ferry and the Golden Arrow boat trains. It became synonymous with elegance with wagon-lits and the Venice Simplon Orient Express. Today it has the Gatwick Express – enough said!

The remaining Southern region termini handle relatively little traffic compared to the 150 million per annum shared between Waterloo and Victoria, but they are closer by a mile or so and therefore more convenient for the East End and new business quarter.

London Bridge is the least impressive of the London termini. From the outside it does not look like a terminus at all; it looks like, and is, a bus station. With high-rise development taking place adjacent to it, the station will soon become another obscure shopping centre which happens to have a station concourse. For a station which handles over 50 million passengers a year, this is an architectural disgrace especially as so many visitors come to London to see London Bridge and Tower Bridge which are immediately adjacent. London Bridge actually claims to be the oldest of the London termini, having been opened in September 1836, but it was such a piecemeal affair that Euston laid claim to that title as London Bridge did not even have a roof when opened to serve the London and Croydon Railway from 1838, with running powers granted to both the London and Brighton Railway and the South Eastern Railway. The original site was soon found to be limiting to the volume of traffic, and a new station was built on a new site in 1844. Due to the merger of various companies, this in turn was demolished and a new station built by 1850, then again in 1864, which is where the present station stands. The grouping brought the station under single ownership, and the lines into it were electrified by 1928. The station suffered bomb damage in the Second World War, and the former hotel, already demoted to railway offices, was demolished altogether. None of the grand Midland Hotel architecture here! Thus it can be seen that there was never any Grand Plan for London Bridge, or indeed for any of the southern stations, unlike the grand buildings north of the Thames. They evolved to fit passenger needs and it seems that they still are, with the removal of Eurostar from Waterloo to St Pancras.

The utilitarian concourse of London Bridge, built by 1978 to British Rail design, is matched by the austere and equally functional appearance of the platforms. There seems to be none of the pride in the structure that exists at, say, Paddington or even Euston, though some authors claim this to be one of the 'best modern reconstructions'. The arched Brighton roof seen to the right of Platform 10 is the only piece of architecture of any elegance which remains.

London Bridge, like Waterloo, has some through lines a link across the Thames, in this case to Cannon Street. It was opened in 1866 to serve the South Eastern Railway and was an elegant design from the outset with two towers either side of a high iron and glass roof. It boasted its own hotel, as all the great stations did, but both suffered bomb damage in the Second World War and the glass roof was lost even though attempts to store it had been made.

Further bombing by the IRA in 1974 did not help the remains of the original structure and the station was closed for five months, the extra traffic being mainly handled by London Bridge. This clearly gave political opportunists the green light, and the permanent closure of Cannon Street was considered.

In the 1950s the original station had largely been demolished in a land grab by an ambitious property developer named John Poulson, who was subsequently found to have corrupted a BR surveyor Graham Tunbridge. This building was eventually demolished, and with the radical political changes of the 1980s with their emphasis on privatisation and profiteering, yet more haggling took place about the demolition of the station for prime office space, in spite of its value to passengers.

Fortunately by 1981 some sense had returned to the property boom era, and the station was retained underneath an office block, but at least with some architectural elegance. The rebuilding stipulated that the line of sight from St Paul's to Tower Bridge should be retained.

Cannon Street concourse and platforms.

The photographs show the two sides of Cannon Street as seen from south of the river.

Above Cannon Street with St Paul's to the west. The original towers have been cleaned and restored.

Right The view of the eastern side with the 'modern' East End.

Continuing round London in a clockwise direction, the smaller station of Fenchurch Street is one of the least accessible and one of the most attractive of the capital's main line stations. It is now in the centre of some of the most expensive land in Britain, being located in the old city, and was the first station to be constructed there, being opened in 1841. One cannot help but observe how short the time span was between the opening of each of the London termini. Again the station soon had more traffic than it could cope with, and was rebuilt in 1854.

The façade is very similar to that of Ipswich station on the Great Eastern Railway, a railway company that made use of the terminus between 1890 and 1920 due to the chronic overcrowding of Liverpool Street three quarters of a mile away. There is no Underground connection.

Opposite from top
Inside, the two main platforms are busy, with increasing usage each year.

The façade of Ipswich which closely resembles that of Fenchurch Street. Ipswich has changed little apart from the overhead catenary. The journey time from Norwich is, however, surprisingly long, and is only a little quicker than the non-stop time in the age of steam. Somehow I expected the much more powerful electric locomotives to decimate the times, with their superior acceleration, but the congested route defeated any such opportunity.

By contrast Liverpool Street has changed beyond all recognition from the smoky 'Cathedral' I had once known and seen on earlier pages of this book. The station was a late starter, but has made up for it since, being the third busiest terminal in London in 2010 with 120 million people using it in that year, surpassed only by Waterloo and Victoria. The station as I knew it is not on the site of the original GER terminal opened in 1840. The new station dates from 1875, and has been largely destroyed a number of times, being bombed in both the First World War (unusually, being the first place in London to be bombed) and the Second World War. Fortunately, the great pillars and superb roof survived and have been incorporated into the new station rebuilt and reopened in 1991. It is all that remains of the elegant Victorian architecture and the wonderful façade of the Great Eastern Hotel. A journey into London Liverpool Street shows how much the modernisation of London has affected the railway.

The railway yard at Colchester is a shadow of its former self in August 2010.

Opposite All that remains of Stratford is the site of the new Olympic stadium while the approach to Liverpool Street is daubed with graffiti and is even more squalid than ever.

The exit from Liverpool Street is as congested as ever, but at least the remnants of the old roof and pillars are still visible, and there is some grandeur left as seen below. The old and new roofs are both visible, and the beautiful wrought ironwork over the taxi rank gives one an impression of what the station once was – although thousands of commuters never looked upwards!

The concourse is now a modern shopping arcade. One has to ask where the platforms are!

Outside it is not obvious that a station is there at all. The young lady, mobile in hand and eating while she crosses a busy Liverpool Street, embraces the culture of the modern city.

The Midland Railway built St Pancras station to avoid the congestion it was experiencing using Euston. St Pancras was a slum area in the mid-1800s and the land was bought cheaply. The station was started in 1864 and completed in 1867 after experiencing many problems with the coffins and remains in the graveyards at the platform end of the station. The grand roof is attributed to William Barlow and remains in place today. The Midland Hotel, opposite below, was designed by George G. Scott, and was opened in 1873. The station remained unchanged until the Midland Hotel was closed in 1935, and used as offices. By 1960 there were proposals to close St Pancras, but the reinstatement of the plans to use it for a European link saved it, and today it is the Eurostar terminal; the interior of the station is considerably altered from Barlow's original train shed.

In the days of steam, St Pancras was always very quiet compared to the traffic in Kings Cross next door. It lacked the glamour, and I have few shots of the magnificent architecture. Perhaps St Pancras is fortunate that the real estate value of the land in the 1960s, coupled with Michael Heseltine's determination to redevelop the East End, reprieved it. Today the modern building is a mixture. The magnificent roof is gazed at by a life-size statue of Sir John Betjeman, who campaigned so hard to save it. (I hope Michael Palin is equally successful with Euston's Doric arch!) Paul Day's statue of the lovers embracing is, I think, a fine piece of work. However, the shopping precinct has the same effect as the one at Liverpool Street – one wonders where the trains are! The Eurostar platforms are so sterile one wonders if anything actually arrives or departs.

Opposite below If Liverpool Street is at the heart of the modern city, St Pancras is struggling to do the same, surrounded as it is with some of the oldest and ugliest of North London's construction. The city has crept eastwards from Euston but the progress from the city side has been slow coming and the proximity of Kings Cross does not help. Nevertheless the old Midland Hotel is as dominant as ever, although spoilt by the hoarding and advertising surrounding its base.

St Pancras shopping precinct –
or is it a station?

Paul Day's statue under the
clock at St Pancras.

Looking like a Hornby model, the Eurostar platforms are protected by a glass screen.

So having started from the oldest terminal in London, and travelling in a clockwise direction in a circle of approximately 4 miles diameter, we come to the youngest of the London termini, Marylebone. The name comes from St Mary's Church on a tributary of the Thames, the River Bourne (and so Mary-le-Bourne), but the station is much more recent having been opened in 1899 as the terminus for the last main line into London, the Great Central. The building has remained unaltered. Inside it has been modernised and has a pleasant concourse but only three operational platforms, with one outside the train shed.

The Great Central operated from High Wycombe, Aylesbury and as far afield as Rugby, Leicester, Nottingham, Sheffield and Manchester; but it will be observed that all these places already had a route into other London termini, even via London Underground, and the line mainly operated hauling freight. The terminus was consequently never very busy, and its parent railway companies varied over the years from LMS to LNER; even the GWR had a part. Marylebone thus became the place for chartered steam specials! The station's fortunes were reversed in the 1980s when large numbers of commuter trains were diverted from Paddington's overstretched terminal and the station now has a healthy future. Let us hope that is true for all of the lines into London.

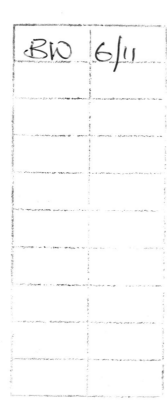

BW	6/11